MARINE FORCE
RECON

LEE SLATER

**Checkerboard
Library**

An Imprint of Abdo Publishing
abdopublishing.com

abdopublishing.com

Published by Abdo Publishing, a division of ABDO, PO Box 398166, Minneapolis, Minnesota 55439.
Copyright © 2016 by Abdo Consulting Group, Inc. International copyrights reserved in all countries.
No part of this book may be reproduced in any form without written permission from the publisher.
Checkerboard Library™ is a trademark and logo of Abdo Publishing.

Printed in the United States of America, North Mankato, Minnesota
102015
012016

THIS BOOK CONTAINS
RECYCLED MATERIALS

Cover Photo: Sgt. Paul Peterson/DVIDS
Interior Photos: Alexander Mitchell/USMC, pp. 11, 28; Anna Albrecht/USMC, p. 9; Austin Long/USMC,
p. 23; Captaindan/Wikipedia, p. 25; Chris Garcia/USMC, p. 17; CIA, p. 24; Danielle Rodrigues/USMC,
p. 22; David Hersey/USMC, p. 12; Elizabeth A. Case/USMC, p. 14; Elize McKelvey/USMC, p. 18; HO/
Reuters/Corbis, pp. 4, 5, 28; Jericho W. Crutcher/USMC, p. 15; Joseph Scanlan/USMC, pp. 6-7,
27; Joshua Murray/USMC, pp. 26, 28; Nicolas von Kospoth, p. 25; PEO Soldier/US Army, p. 25;
Shutterstock, pp. 4, 6, 8, 10, 12, 14, 16, 18, 20, 21, 22, 24, 25, 26; Sullivan Laramie/USMC, p. 16;
Tyler Andersen/USMC, p. 13; US Air Force, p. 24; US Army, p. 25; USMC, pp. 8, 10, 28

Content Developer: Nancy Tuminelly
Design: Anders Hanson, Mighty Media, Inc.
Editor: Liz Salzmann

Library of Congress Cataloging-in-Publication Data
Slater, Lee, 1969-
  Marine Force Recon / Lee Slater.
     pages cm. -- (Special ops)
  Includes index.
  ISBN 978-1-62403-970-6
1. United States. Marine Corps. Force Reconnaissance--Juvenile literature. 2. United States.
Marine Corps--Commando troops--Juvenile literature. I. Title.
  VE23.S57 2015
  359.9'64130973--dc23
                     2015026594

CONTENTS

CHAPTER 1

A MISSION TO
CAPTURE
PIRATES

On September 9, 2010, Force Recon marines went on a predawn **raid**. Somali pirates had captured the German-owned cargo ship *Magellan Star*. Somalia's coast is on a busy shipping route. Pirates often tried to capture ships, and it was hard to stop them.

The *USS Dubuque (left)* and Turkish ship *TCG Gökçeada (background)* provided protection and support during the rescue of the *Magellan Star (right)*.

The pirates were well armed. They were ready to shoot anyone who got in their way. The *Magellan Star* had a crew of 11. The crew members saw the pirates start to board the ship. Then the crew members locked themselves in the engine room. From there, they were able to call for help.

The Force Recon marines snuck up on the *Magellan Star* in inflatable boats.

The US Marines, the US Navy, and the Turkish Navy responded. They worked together to form a rescue plan. The commanders received important information from the *Magellan Star*'s crew. They knew how many pirates were on board and where they were located.

Marines with 2nd Platoon, Force Reconnaissance Company sped toward the *Magellan Star*. The marines climbed ladders to board the ship. The pirates were surprised and outnumbered. They surrendered and the ship's crew was saved. The mission was a complete success, and not one shot was fired.

RECON?

Marine Force Recon is a special operations unit of the US military. *Recon* is short for *reconnaissance* (rih-KAH-nuh-zuhns). This is the act of gathering information about an enemy. Recon work requires patience and secrecy. It also requires excellent observation and communication skills.

Recon soldiers sneak into enemy territory. They observe what is happening.

Force Recon marines observe enemy activities in remote areas. From there, they radio information to their commander.

They work in small teams so they are less likely to be noticed. The soldiers report useful information to their commanders. The information is called intelligence.

The commanders use intelligence from Force Recon to plan missions. Knowing more about the enemy helps missions be more effective. Good

intelligence also helps avoid mistakes. In war, a mistake can cause unnecessary deaths.

Usually, Force Recon is the first special operations team to arrive in a trouble spot. It is sent in ahead of any troops. This is called being forward-**deployed**. The team's soldiers go deep inside enemy territory. They are often many miles from the closest support teams. Their survival depends on remaining hidden and undetected.

CHAPTER 3

FOUNDING OF
MARINE
FORCE RECON

The roots of Force Recon can be traced back to the Amphibious Reconnaissance **Battalion**. It was active during **World War II**. At that time, the battalion played an important role in observing enemy beaches.

The battalion's duties were to scout on and near beaches. Its men cleared obstacles and watched for enemy activity. Information from the battalion helped improve battle **strategies** and safeguard troops.

General Lemuel Shepherd

In the 1950s, General Lemuel Shepherd was the officer in charge of the Marine Corps. He created Marine Corps Test Unit One. Major Bruce F. Meyers led the unit. Meyers organized the testing of recon methods. He wanted to find better ways for men to get deep into enemy territory.

Meyers's unit tested new **parachuting** methods. It used different kinds of planes. The unit also developed a way to leave and enter a submarine while it is underwater. When a sub surfaces, it is very noticeable.

Today's Force Recon marines continue to use water insertions and other methods to enter enemy territory.

Being able to leave the sub without it surfacing let recon soldiers get closer to shore undetected.

As a result of these tests, the 1st Force Reconnaissance Company was formed in 1957. Meyers was its first commanding officer. The 2nd Force Reconnaissance Company followed in 1958.

CHAPTER 4

WHAT DOES
MARINE
FORCE RECON DO?

Force Recon trains for air, land, and sea insertions and extractions. Insertion is the act of getting into enemy territory without being seen. Extraction is the act of getting safely out of enemy territory without being captured.

During some green operations, Force Recon marines swim ashore. Then they try to move quietly across the beach.

Force Recon marines enter and search buildings during black operations.

Force Recon performs both green operations and black operations. Green operations focus on observing and gathering intelligence. Black operations require direct action. This includes executing **raids**. Force Recon supports different marine task forces. Sometimes Force Recon is part of a joint effort. It works with other branches of the military.

The success of Force Recon missions depends on the men being able to get along with each other. They spend months training together as a team. They learn to communicate with each other without saying a word.

Force Recon marines are highly trained, intelligent, skilled, and brave. Becoming a Force Recon soldier is very difficult. Only a very small percentage of candidates complete the training.

CHAPTER 6

BEFORE THE REAL
TRAINING
BEGINS

All marines attend Marine Recruit Training and the School of **Infantry**. There, they learn to use weapons of all kinds. They become excellent soldiers. Marines who want to join Force Recon go through additional training.

During RIP, marines hike 10 miles (16 km) carrying a 50-pound (22.7 kg) rucksack.

The first step in joining Force Recon is the Recon Indoctrination Program (RIP). RIP is an extreme test of physical and mental fitness. In this program, marines swim, run, and march. They do pull-ups, push-ups, and sit-ups. RIP also includes challenging obstacle courses.

Marines try to do as many sit-ups as they can in two minutes during RIP.

All this and more takes place in just 48 hours! If a candidate scores well enough on the physical tests, he undergoes a **psychological** interview. A candidate who has a poor attitude or who doesn't work well on a team may be rejected.

RIP is designed to be very difficult to pass. The success rate is always less than 50 percent. Only the most physically and mentally tough soldiers can become Force Recon marines.

CHAPTER 7

FORCE
RECON
TRAINING

Candidates who pass RIP then take the Basic Reconnaissance Course (BRC). BRC has three **phases**. The first two phases are taught at Camp Pendleton, California. The third phase is held in Coronado, California.

The first phase lasts four weeks. It focuses on individual physical skills such as swimming, running, and obstacle courses. This phase also covers land navigation, communications, and weapons training.

The second phase lasts three weeks. It concentrates on small-unit **tactics** and mission planning. This phase includes a nine-day practice recon mission.

The third phase lasts two weeks. This phase focuses on water-based missions. Candidates learn water recon, boat operations, and water navigation.

Marines blow holes in boards during explosives training.

BRC includes swimming 2,000 yards (1,829 m) in uniform while towing an 80-pound (36.3 kg) bag.

Candidates who pass BRC are qualified as Force Recon marines. But their training is far from over. There are many advanced training courses they can take. Some of the advanced courses are offered by the US Marines. Others are in other branches of the US military.

Advanced courses include:

- US Marine Corps Combatant Diver Course
- US Marine Corps Scout **Sniper** Course
- Navy Survival, **Evasion**, Resistance, Escape (SERE) Training
- Army Airborne School (Jump Master Training)
- Army Ranger School

CREED

The **motto** of Force Recon is "Swift, Silent, Deadly." Force Recon marines are always ready to go and are swift in reaching the target area. They enter enemy territory silently by **parachuting**, rafting, or swimming in. They also travel on foot. The mission depends on them not being seen or heard. When direct action is needed, these warriors are trained to use deadly force.

The Force Recon Creed expresses beliefs held by every Force Recon soldier. These powerful words inspire them in war and in everyday life. Note that the first letters of the sections spell RECON.

Marines prepare for action with a speed-reload drill.

THE FORCE RECON CREED

REALIZING it is my choice and my choice alone to be a Reconnaissance Marine, I accept all challenges **involved** with this profession. Forever shall I strive to maintain the tremendous reputation of those who went before me.

EXCEEDING beyond the limitations set down by others shall be my goal. Sacrificing personal comforts and **dedicating** myself to the completion of the reconnaissance mission shall be my life. Physical fitness, mental attitude, and high **ethics**—The title of Recon Marine is my honor.

CONQUERING all obstacles, both large and small, I shall never quit. To quit, to surrender, to give up is to fail. To be a Reconnaissance Marine is to **surpass** failure; to overcome, to adapt and to do whatever it takes to complete the mission.

ON the battlefield, as in all areas of life, I shall stand tall above the competition. Through professional pride, **integrity**, and teamwork, I shall be the example for all Marines to **emulate**.

NEVER shall I forget the principles I accepted to become a Reconnaissance Marine. Honor, **Perseverance**, Spirit, and Heart. A Recon Marine can speak without saying a word and achieve what others can only imagine.

ON THE JOB

Force Recon operates all over the world. Force Recon marines can get to trouble spots on short notice. They usually arrive under the cover of darkness. They make a silent entrance by air, sea, or land.

Operation Enduring Freedom began in 2001 and lasted for more than 13 years. During this campaign, Force Recon performed important missions in the mountains of Afghanistan. The troops already there were having a hard time getting supplies. The enemy had hidden explosive devices along the supply roads. Soldiers were being killed, and the troops were running out of supplies.

Force Recon marines came swiftly and silently to the rescue. They hid in the rugged mountains and watched where the enemy placed explosives. Then they reported this information back to the commanders.

The commanders told the drivers of the supply trucks where the explosives were. The drivers were then able to avoid the explosives. The enemy was outsmarted and the supplies got through to the troops.

FORCE RECON GLOBAL ACTION

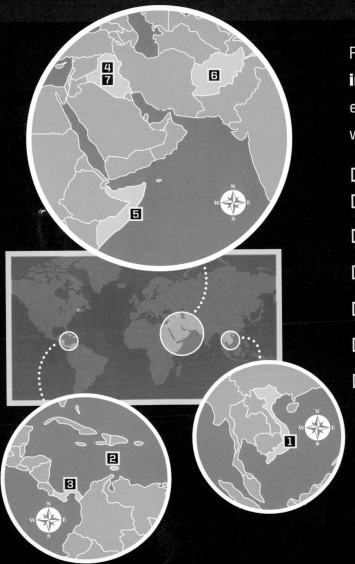

Force Recon has been **involved** in many military engagements since the unit was established in 1957.

1. VIETNAM WAR (1965-1975)
2. OPERATION URGENT FURY, GRENADA (1983)
3. OPERATION JUST CAUSE, PANAMA (1989-1990)
4. OPERATION DESERT STORM, IRAQ (1990-1991)
5. OPERATION RESTORE HOPE, SOMALIA (1992-1993)
6. OPERATION ENDURING FREEDOM, AFGHANISTAN (2001-2014)
7. OPERATION IRAQI FREEDOM, IRAQ (2003-2010)

CHAPTER 10

THE
GHILLIE
SUIT

Force Recon **snipers** wear ghillie (GIH-lee) suits so they can blend into their surroundings. A ghillie suit is a special kind of **camouflage** clothing. The human form is very easily recognizable. A ghillie suit disguises the sniper's outline so he's harder to see.

A sniper often makes a ghillie suit for his rifle.
It disguises the rifle's straight lines.

The grasses on a ghillie suit move just like the surrounding plants. This disguises the marine's movements as he sneaks past a lookout.

Ready-made ghillie suits are available, but many **snipers** choose to make their own. To make a ghillie suit, a sniper usually starts with an old uniform. He pads the front of the suit. When on a mission, a sniper sometimes spends hours or even days lying on the ground. The padding protects him from hard, uncomfortable surfaces.

The sniper then attaches **camouflage** netting to the suit. Finally, he attaches strips of fabric, twigs, leaves, and other materials to the netting. It's important for the sniper to use things that match the area where he plans to hide.

CHAPTER 11

FORCE

RECON

GEAR

Force Recon marines use many different tools and weapons. Their gear can change based on the needs of the mission. Force Recon marines carefully choose what to bring on each mission to ensure its success.

Reconnaissance Gear

laser marker

GPS receiver

long-range communications radio

night vision scope

observation scope

Weapons

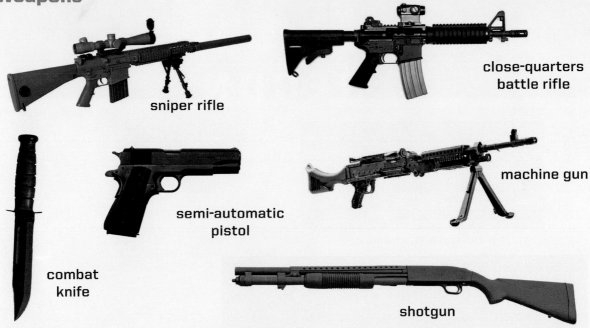

sniper rifle

close-quarters
battle rifle

semi-automatic
pistol

machine gun

combat
knife

shotgun

Accessories & Supplies

extra ammunition

night vision
goggles

optical sight
for a rifle

grenade launcher
for a rifle

CHAPTER 12

THE FUTURE OF
FORCE
RECON

Today, Force Recon also plays an important role in training foreign militaries. Its expertise is in demand. Force Recon works with the militaries of countries such as Korea and Australia, training their soldiers to fight **terrorism**.

Even while training foreign soldiers, Force Recon marines are always gathering intelligence. With the right information, attacks can be prevented and enemy leaders captured. Fighting

Force Recon marines use different extraction and insertion methods, including insertion by parachute.

global **terrorism** is one of Force Recon's most important tasks. Force Recon marines are at work right now, all over the world. For safety reasons, they keep exactly where they operate a secret.

Force Recon will continue to **specialize** in intelligence gathering, but still perform some direct operations. Force Recon skills are especially useful in missions at sea. Force Recon marines go wherever there's a need for men who are "swift, silent, and deadly."

Force Recon marines are always training to keep up their physical fitness. They have to stay strong enough to carry their huge packs. A pack can weigh more than 100 pounds (45 kg)!

TIMELINE

1941–1945

The Amphibious Reconnaissance Battalion operates during World War II.

1958

The 2nd Force Reconnaissance Company is activated.

1980s

Force Recon marines are involved in Operation Urgent Fury and Operation Just Cause.

1957

The 1st Force Reconnaissance Company is activated.

1965–1974

Force Recon marines fight in the Vietnam War.

1990s

Force Recon marines are involved in Operation Desert Storm and Operation Restore Hope.

2000s

Force Recon marines are involved in Operation Enduring Freedom and Operation Iraqi Freedom.

2010

Force Recon marines help rescue the crew of the *Magellan Star*.

EXTREME FACTS

- Marine Force Recon has no official emblem.

- Force Recon marines must be able to swim 30 yards underwater without coming up for air.

- All Force Recon operators are required to be expert **parachutists**.

- As part of a swim test, Force Recon candidates must tread water for 40 minutes. They are fully clothed and must pass around weights and rifles during the test.

- The Marvel comic book character The Punisher (Frank Castle) was a **Vietnam War**-era Force Recon marine.

GLOSSARY

battalion – a military unit that includes two or more smaller units.

camouflage – relating to hiding or disguising something by covering it up or changing its appearance.

color-blind – partially or totally unable to tell one color from another.

dedicate – to commit oneself to a goal or a way of life.

deploy – to spread out and organize in a battle formation.

elite – of or relating to the best of a class.

emulate – to try to copy or be better than someone else.

ethics – the rules of moral conduct followed by a person or group.

evasion – the act of escaping or avoiding something.

fluent – able to speak clearly and easily in a certain language.

infantry – soldiers trained and organized to fight on foot.

integrity – the state or act of being honest and sincere.

involve – 1. to require certain parts or actions. 2. to take part in something.

motto – a word or sentence that describes a guiding principle.

parachute – to jump out of an aircraft and use a parachute to fall slowly to the ground. A parachute is an umbrella-like device consisting of fabric from which a person or object is suspended.

WEBSITES

To learn more about Special Ops, visit **booklinks.abdopublishing.com**. These links are routinely monitored and updated to provide the most current information available.

perseverance – the quality that allows a person to keep trying to do something even though it is difficult.

phase – a step or stage of a process.

psychological – related to someone's mind and behavior.

raid – a surprise attack.

sniper – someone who shoots at an enemy from a hidden place far away.

specialize – to limit business or operations to a specific area.

strategy – a careful plan or method.

surpass – to be greater, better, or stronger than something or someone.

tactics – the science of moving military forces in battle.

terrorism – the use of violence to threaten people or governments.

Vietnam War – from 1957 to 1975. A long, failed attempt by the United States to stop North Vietnam from taking over South Vietnam.

World War II – from 1939 to 1945, fought in Europe, Asia, and Africa. Great Britain, France, the United States, the Soviet Union, and their allies were on one side. Germany, Italy, Japan, and their allies were on the other side.

INDEX